contents

Who Would Be Dumb Enough to Be a Salesperson?...2

Most Have Been Selling Since Diapers...9

Let's Talk More About Fear...15

February...19

Chameleons, Predators, and Prey...28

Suspects or Prospects...42

There Are No Slow Seasons...50

Your BIGGEST Opponent is Undefeated...56

Is Selling Speed-Dating or Courtship...60

Mr. Support Person...63

Conclusion: Go Make Some Money...67

introduction

I have been chasing numbers for cash and prizes for over 35 years. It's debatable whether I am the best, but without a doubt I have been successful, even across products. For about the last ten of those thirty-five-plus years, I have wanted to assemble my random thoughts about my time in the "convincing and positioning business," which is my fancy way of describing the craft of selling.

I have learned some hard lessons, along with many that were amusing and Insightful, about people and perceptions. I have had the pleasure and displeasure of working with many bosses of varying degrees of ability and with salespeople who had the same sorts of advantages and opportunities. I am not so naïve to think that I have not been looked upon by some in the same regard, but I am too egotistical to admit that it may be true. However, it is easy to determine what has been most enjoyable to me, and that would without a doubt be my many co-workers. Please do not misunderstand this to mean that I have not enjoyed interacting with most of my customers and media types. I can honestly say that some customers have been an absolute joy to work and grow with, and some have even been iconic in their category. When comparing clients to co-workers, let me state the obvious: the biggest difference is that many clients are far more unpredictable because you live with those you work with.

I was fortunate to have honed many of my meager sales skills toiling in retail for ten years. Ten long years. That is three thousand six hundred and fifty days. I obviously did not work every day. It just felt like it. My complaining aside, it taught me the fine art of instant tolerance and credibility, which are not particularly easy to earn when you are a black man. I attended the most integrated high school in Philadelphia, which was a stark contrast to my neighborhood. I also played sports year-round. This allowed exposure and interaction with people who were different from me and generally not as poor. As a selling professional, one that became adept at using a neutral, non-ethnic voice, often I'd get that look when I walked into a business meeting. But it was not solely my David Allen Grier white guy voice that surprised people. It was also my last name, which to some sounds Italian. Relax. Before you think this is going to be a "I was the coal in the snow" or a "too dark for the house and too light for the field" book, let me say this book is all about my observations and not my ethnicity, although that played a factor in some of what I have learned and will share. There is no white guilt associated in this text. I promise. I will offer a similar promise if you are black and think that I may just recommend that you cannot be yourself. This is NOT a "poor me, selling as a black person is hard" story, by any means. Yes, selling as a black person is hard. But selling is hard no matter your ethnicity, color, or religion.

The name of this book, Who Would Be Dumb Enough to Be a Salesperson? is not intended to be merely a question. It is a challenge, and a query. The very term *sales* conjure up images of that fast-talking guy who only tells you enough so you make a decision that solely benefits him. That you have been tricked, bamboozled, and fooled in some manner. That they spun a yarn meant to dupe you. Does this happen? Only to those too trusting. Hey, we all have trusting days. Do some sales types believe this methodology works? None who have been in it longer than for a cup of coffee in any one industry. No one wants to be sold anything. Not really. Did you <u>buy</u> your car, or was it <u>sold</u> to you? I will bet that the overwhelming majority will say they bought their car. Being sold something rarely is how anyone remembers the transaction. And absolutely no one wants to be misled to make a bad buying decision ever. They may enjoy the cat-and-mouse sales game, but it's usually because they believe themselves to be the cat, firmly in-charge of the game. Does selling sound like a day at the beach for a seller? It rarely is ever easy, and the problem is usually the product, the pitch, or what is between one's ears. Sometimes all three. There are books out there (along with other media) that will talk about relationships and others will focus on the follow-up. Some will include a goofy formula that is a "can't miss" approach. There are many that attempt to be a catch-all. Some are very good but not necessarily because of the methodology within them. Sometimes, it is because a sales book, any sales book, can be a tool to develop confidence and a mindset. This text attempts to minimally give you some insight on whether selling professionally is for you, and perhaps it will make you just a bit better at it. Scratch that last line. It *will* make you better, and taller. I sound like a sales guy, right?

I have tried to keep it short. Who wants to read *War and Peace* about this subject? Why not go get a wisdom tooth removed or do a ton of other things that are a lot more fun? Besides, selling is hard. Selling sucks. Who is dumb enough to want to? Reading some blockhead's perspective, even this blockhead, about selling is often harder. Big, audacious yawn. There is a saying in the martial arts that talks about how every person walks alone, or some such drivel. Despite my minimizing it, I believe it to be a very true statement, and it is just as true in selling or operating in a sales environment. Many organizations, mine included, have all sorts of resources. But at the end of the day, it always depends upon how effective the seller is in positioning the proper opportunity with the correct buyer. Wait...I am jumping ahead, stating the obvious. If I do not know you and am not related to you, I can only assume that you are one of three things: a successful seller trying to be better, a not so successful seller trying to be better, or someone interested in selling for a living The title is meant to scare off the weak and intimidated. The harsh reality is that selling professionally is not for everyone. If you lack the will but have some skill, you can fake it for a time, but not forever. If this sounds callous or dismissive, it was meant to be. Selling just is not for everyone. As Jenny famously once said, "Run, Forrest."

If you don't want to make a better than average living, or if you would prefer to remain in a safe, stable, mouse-on-a-wheel job, it is ok that you have bought this book. You will at least learn more about why you don't want to sell for a living, further validating why selling is hard and not for you.

Whether you are a seasoned pro or someone considering going into professional sales, you have made a good decision in buying this book. If not for you, do it for me for having the heart to write it. Besides, buying this book will make you a better person, it will help you lose weight, and may even make you witty. Well, perhaps I am over promising here and am really speaking in jest.

chapter 01

Most Have Been Selling Since Diapers

No one was a little kid who aspired to be a salesperson when they grew up. They had their sights set on being a cowboy, doctor, astronaut, firemen, police officer, or president even. The world is full of salespeople. But if you asked the average person if they are able or willing to sell, you would get a flat-out unambiguous, firmly stated no. I believe that sales and public speaking fall into similar boxes. It is said that some people would rather die than speak publicly. Really? They would prefer or are less afraid of death than standing in front of a bunch of strangers having to speak? Seeking approval or acceptance about what you are trying to communicate is scary. Asking someone to trust what you are saying or asking them to commit finances or a commitment to your position can be intimidating...but you will live. Even a hard-nosed sales type like me understands the fear part.

The displeasing thought of selling is partially why you hear so many titles for sales professionals: advisor, consultant, advocate, business development. Regardless of ridiculous title, everyone usually falls into the profession through circumstances based on needing a job. They generally did not plan to be in this aspect at all. Back to titles for a second...why not convincer, hypnotist, or desperado?

I am always amazed when I hear someone say they could never, ever sell. I have heard this from professionals in all walks of life. A lawyer trying to secure a client is sales. You have heard them in commercials and screaming from painted ads on park benches. You probably heard this also from family and friends, including maybe from your own mouth at some point in your life, stated not so elegantly. It is always the look-away followed by "I could never be in sales." But is that true, or are they simply "selling" themselves short?

The fact is that most people have been selling for their entire lives. It began when they were young and continued all through school, work, and unconsciously every day of their lives. It's happening constantly and within the most common of circumstances, without even a second thought. That someone isn't asking for money or trust has little to do with it. In most situations, it is amazingly subtle and sophisticated with body language and voice inflection. Professional sales types do it all the time, unwittingly. Some even in matters of love. Selling is a complicated skill that can indeed be used for money, love, influence, favor, and otherwise. Superhuman? For some, maybe.

How is it that a person can sell for their entire existence, non-professionally, for all sorts of things, but not have a clue? Let's consider some points that may be familiar to you. Depending on your age group, it may have started with trying to convince mom of buying that Barbie, G.I. Joe, or Ninja Turtle. It may have progressed when trying to convince dad to use the car or perhaps getting that special someone to go to the movies. From there, it may have been convincing that sorority to accept you, trying to get a professor to give you a better grade or landing that job or promotion. It could be the daily negotiation with the kids, the significant other or spouse, or even the dog. Have you ever tried to talk your way out of a ticket? Get a second job interview? Get a free upgrade in a hotel? Selling is what you were doing! It is all selling, and there is usually some sort of commission paid for closing the sale. And make no mistake that some are extremely good at it and are almost as equally unaware. Are you one of the zombie sellers? Those of you not in sales, do you honestly believe that it is only your Hollywood looks and winning smile that has made the difference? Maybe. The fact is most people have been in sales mode constantly and often blissfully unaware. For those of us who do it professionally, well, it is an occupational hazard. What separates the conscious professional and the unknowing citizen is simply the awareness of a financial goal. Many may see salespeople as having some special skill with a foundation built with leather-like thick skin to handle rejection and are likely unaware of their own ability. We often say they are "natural-born sellers." However, this is usually not the case. Conscious professionals are painfully aware of this fact. Amateurs, if I may be so bold, are just as deliberate and enjoy the challenge until they get the absolute no. Professionals consider how they can pitch it differently. Generally, the difference in selling, whether it may be professionally or otherwise, is the motivation and desires of the person doing the convincing. But more than often, it simply comes down to wanting to win. What there is to win matters not. This is an important point that divides sales contenders from sales pretenders, and I am being serious. It could be as basic as being elected to the church council or as big as securing a seven-figure deal. There is literally no difference emotionally, especially for anyone who wants to win. This is the reason that most sales teams have sales contests. It is to capitalize and bring forth that passion that is present in all great sellers. If a professional seller made a lot of money, but finished at the bottom on their team, they would not be happy, or at least should not be. The money and success are a byproduct of the desire to win, to be the best. If you are ok with *not* winning, do yourself a favor and stay out of sales. But if you have any drive to be at the top, or are willing to work hard to be among the elite of your team, you can be a successful seller. The next time you hear someone groaning on about the fact that they could never sell in a million years, just smile. If you want to make them give you a double-take and stutter, just ask them who they are trying to sell that to. See if they get the irony.

Let's Talk More About Fear

Fear and sales should never be said in the same sentence. Let's have a look at what fear is, as described in a Google search: Fear is the most general term and implies anxiety and usually loss of courage. Fear of the unknown dread usually adds the idea of intense reluctance to face or meet a person or situation and suggests aversion as well as anxiety. That is a pretty dark description of a human emotion, but what does it have to do with sales? What so many people are afraid of is rejection, if not the mere idea of having to ask someone for something?

Real fear is having to go to school every day worrying about being beat up by a gang or even getting killed. Depending on where someone goes to school, maybe it's the mean girls. Or maybe it's an inappropriate teacher or adult figure. How about those millions of people who

are without food security for themselves or their children?

How about that person who needs to nail that interview or they could very well lose their home or car? Without making this depressing, what I am driving at is that selling should not inspire fear because there are plenty of things in the world to be afraid of.

Sales is preparation and perspiration, in varying measures. When you combine these elements after qualifying a prospect, your formula of success is based upon the law of large numbers. That law, simply stated, is rooted in the math theory that the more prospects you ask, the greater your frequency of success. It is not a complicated approach, but it is pointless without the right product for that potential client's need. Anything less, and you should be petrified by fear. If you have the right product, have properly qualified the client, and you can position the opportunity correctly, you should not be fearful at all. You should be fearless.

If fear is overstated, maybe the proper term and feeling that you (or a friend) have is anxiety. You or your friend have likely talked yourself into failure and are thinking and considering what would be the fallout of failure. You cannot win worried or afraid. You are likely to come off like lieutenant Columbo, and his character was not someone that I would regard as a selling professional. He was one helluva TV cop, as he was smart with a great memory. But he was rarely decisive and confident, until the end. You must maintain that air of confidence, even if you are scared to death asking for someone's trust. Don't be afraid because you are not selling.

February

This chapter has nothing to do with the month. Coincidentally, it the shortest month of the year, which is also Black History Month. Who negotiated that deal anyway? Again, I pledged a non-ethnic driven text, but this is a subject that I need to address for those of you who may fall within this segment. Let me get right into it. Selling as a black person is extremely difficult. The world sees black men often as dangerous thugs they need to fear. We are all without manners and are in perpetual pursuit of white women. This is not hyperbole. The media, the justice system, and other black people all put us in a bad light for a host of reasons. Often the first order of business is to surmount the preconceived notions that many of your co-workers may harbor. So often, many just aren't exposed to other kinds of people. I spent a brief time selling life insurance. I had a license and was connected to a guy who is still a prominent agent in the Philadelphia area. I met a friend's agent at their house once, and he was driving a convertible Mercedes. Huh? What's this about, and how can I get in on it? My broker, who was also a seller, would give me absolutely terrible leads. Despite this challenge, I still managed to close a few here and there, but I had to venture into some areas that weren't the most receptive or ethnically diverse to do so. I once did a visit in the Franklin Mills Mall area, which is in the northern section of Philadelphia. Back then, it was all white, and not very friendly toward anyone different. I did not care. I showed up, after dutifully calling and setting an appointment, on time and in a tie. With my Wayne

Brady smile, I marched up and rang the doorbell. A chubby, casually dressed man in his twenties answered the door. He looked at me with furrowed eyebrows as he asked me, for the second time, why I was there. He retreated inside, leaving me standing outside, only to return alone to ask me to show him what I had. I didn't believe he was the one I had set the appointment with, but it was clear that I would not have access to their home. So, I did what any good selling professional would do. I made the pitch right on their front stoop. It was horrible. It was humiliating. But what did I have to lose? And guess what happened? Wrong, as I know that many of you default to happy endings. I never got the deal! Big surprise. This was over 30 years ago. It didn't dissuade me from selling. It just reminded me how steep the hill could be for a guy like me. Although I never got the opportunity to read body language and pivot based on questions, what I learned that day was to never forget what people see and never let anything of the sort stop me from trying. I have sold to all types of people of different persuasions, and if I did not have the right product to fulfill a need or desire, I didn't get the sale. That's how it goes, and it's the way it should work. Unfortunately, some will never hear a word you say because they are unable to get past how you look. Get over it.

I once had a co-worker, an older man back in the 1980s, compliment me because I wasn't lazy and shiftless as what may have been a prevailing thought among his peers about other black men. "Thanks," was my response. What could I say? A female co-worker once asked me how many gold chains I own. Seriously, gold chains? For that one I didn't have a reply. These incidents are literally three decades apart. The first occurred during the GH Bush administration. Both were just as startling. I have others, but enough already.

Some black women are saddled with a different set of challenges, which this statement makes no attempt to discount in any way at all. Often, with even the slightest willingness to stand-up for themselves, they are labeled as being angry or moody. It is generally a no-win situation. Sometimes, the only choices are being docile or forever labeled with the scarlet "A" for attitude. There is a reason that sassy black women did so well on television in the 1970s and 80s. People thought they were funny. Shows like That's My Mama, with a witty mom with an attitude, and The Jefferson's, which included a smart-mouthed maid and neighbor. Remember Nell Carter in Gimmel a Break? Black, sassy and tough on TV is firmly in America's subconscious. You cannot allow this perception to hinder you.

No matter the gender, the first thing is to recognize that these challenges exist and may surface whenever you encounter someone new. It will not matter how charming, smart or highly educated you are or how successful you have been to that point in your career. Despite whatever injustices you believed have occurred in history, do everything right in your life, including not being a caricature. You will still constantly need to prove that you aren't "one of them." The last sentence will no doubt be inflammatory to some of you, but just get over it. There isn't a single person reading this who does not understand where I am coming from, offensive to some as these words may be.

Sorry, I have one more. This is a good one, and unfortunately, timely. A boss once told me that a priest he'd been friends with for many years refused to wear his collar because of the stigma associated with the priesthood. He had received so many negative reactions in his encounters over the years that not wearing his identifying collar just made getting around and interacting with people so much easier. I can understand that, I told him. I followed with how that reminded me so much of being a person of color, but that we have no collar that we can simply chose not to wear. He roared with laughter having played college basketball and having been exposed to black people. He very much got the irony of my point and heartily acknowledged it. You will need to stand firmly on how you see yourself and what you are about. It's ok to like fried chicken and rap music. KFC doesn't just sell to black people. And every other car that goes by me with rap music has a non-minority driving. These points are not what I am talking about. Simply put, you need to not only be good.

You will need to be better by deeds, actions, and most importantly, results. Your mission isn't to prove that you aren't from a fatherless home or that you are a parolee. Your goal is to win. You will need to ignore the slights, real or perceived. It is also important not to see a white sheet under every shirt. Some people are fearful because they've interacted with very few people different from themselves, and they don't know how to not be offensive. It typically is not conscious. If you are hyper-sensitive in that you see racism in everything, you will not fare well. Some will be intentional.

All that you have in the eyes of most people are the things that YOU put out in the world, hopefully changing and countering perceptions one at a time by how you comport yourself. These actions should be in the normal course of business, and intentional but not burdensome. If that is too much, don't sell professionally. If you can handle it, when it is all said and done, people will only see you as green. What I believe had a positive and pivotal role in helping me not carry around a lot of racial baggage was encountering other black people who automatically saw the disadvantage in everything. In some of their minds they were doomed because the world had already condemned them to not be worthy, so working hard was pointless. Trying to be the best would not result in living better. My neighborhood in the rough-and-tumble of south Philadelphia was in a housing project. That scene was right out of a Good Times episode in terms of diversity. As I said in the last chapter, I had the good fortune of playing organized sports year-round while in high school. This allowed me to be exposed and to interact with people who were different from me, and not just by ethnicity. I knew what the sting of racism felt like, but up to that point, mostly from strangers. In high school, I went to the part that was sectioned off for the "smart kids" in a different building. I got to see racism up close that was both obvious and subtle, from strangers and from those thought to be friends. I learned to ignore what did not serve me or did not prepare me for those opportunities when encountering people. This may sound a little disconnected, but think about it? If you were rude, or seem bigoted, I just made a mental note and disregarded it, and if possible, I disregarded your very existence. I decided somewhere to take people as they were and not to assume the worse. Boy, did that help me be a sales guy.

No matter how well you do, someone will remind you directly or accidently of your ethnicity. The way to remove any sting is to never forget who you are and that there are perceptions, no matter how hard you have tried to contradict them. Purposefully, or inadvertently, people will always hang this fact around your neck like a yolk. Smile. Keep your back straight and head up. You cannot be bothered with trying to fix everyone. Your mission is the money. The good news is that sales is the great equalizer, especially when you are on a team. If you choose to disregard every word you read in this book, rest assured that if you are the best producer, your manager will love you to death, even if you are blue. Whatever your ethnicity or gender, be the best (or always strive to be) and you will be valued. Out-hustle. Out-work. If you understand the mission, go after it. If you don't, find out. Your family heritage will come a distant second, assuming of course that you are not a difficult person to manage. That is another topic. If you routinely knock them dead, that may not matter either.

chapter 04

Chameleons, Predators, and Prey

The world is full of specialists. You have doctors and medical professionals for almost every situation and/or part of the body from physical therapists to vascular surgeons to ENTs to acupuncturists. At the Olympics, there are sprinters who defy human capabilities by covering a short amount of space in an incredibly short amount of time. There are high jumpers who jump literally above their own height unaided. There are those who are not fleet of foot over short distances but can cover miles and barely look winded afterward. Who runs a marathon not at gunpoint? I could go on about hammer throwers, shot-putters, and walkers. You will notice that I did not list long jumpers or hurdlers, as many are sprinters also, but you get the point. Then there are the absolutely very best all-around athletes in the decathletes and heptathletes, but they contradict my point (contradicting your own point is not a mistake a good salesperson makes very often). When you consider other sports, there are pitchers who only pitch in between the starters and closers, often called set-up men. I could talk about goalies in various sports or place kickers in American football. There are plenty of examples that I could name across all walks of life and in many non-athletic professions. To be a great seller means a lot more than simply having the ability and fortitude to ask for the order or to close a deal. These attributes are certainly invaluable. Being a great seller sometimes means being a bartender with or without a bar as some solely want you to listen to whatever is happening in their world. Your skill here is in your patience. Some may want you to make them feel superior, whether they are or are not an influencer or a true decision maker. Your skill here is in your patience. Some may want you to tell them what to do just for the opportunity to contradict your recommendations. Yes, this really happens. Your skill here is in your patience. You could find yourself being a spiritual advisor of sorts, a counselor, a consultant, a whipping boy or girl, depending on what may be required that given day. Again, your skill here is in your patience.

Sales types are often characterized as being a great deal like the lizard this chapter is named for. Of course, and in case you missed it, it is not a lizard in a bad sense. There is no denying that the chameleon is a fascinating and a highly adaptable specimen of the animal kingdom. What does this have to do with being a successful seller, you ask? Being highly adaptable in having the ability to facilitate conversations, although at times admittedly shallow, on almost any subject imaginable, and often with an abstract stranger. Coupled with the skill to change and blend into many situations, and well, there you have it. To me, those sound like skill sets that could serve many roles and situations, and they often do. The goal is building a level of trust while also being mildly entertaining, which could come in a varied mix, given the who and where. Again, skill sets that could serve many roles, but especially sales. This is not to say that all are entertaining, as some can be Joe Friday with a "just the facts ma'am" approach. But most sales professionals you meet are just not that way. They are charming and typically on the light side. Sure, some talk too much and most are skilled, experienced, and talented complainers with probably more per capita than any other profession. Salespeople will cry with a loaf of bread under each arm, bitching because they can't reach the loaf at their feet. Key to our ability to blend in is our skill at interacting and charm. I am not speaking of coming off like you are lonely. What I mean by charm is seeming interested without appearing nosey. To hone my charm skills, when I was a full-time seller, I often would practice on people, engaging them in conversation that ultimately was aimed at getting them to talk about their favorite and most familiar subject: themselves. I still do this on occasion, just for fun. A few years ago, I attended a party at an event that was honoring a donor whom I was professionally connected to. The room was mostly filled with academics who had no idea that there was a chameleon among them, namely me. And it never (ever) hurts when there is an open bar. Within an hour's time, someone told me that the organization's president was announcing his departure the next day. Another told me that they were considering expanding their organization. I also learned one or two personal items the person had no reason to share with a stranger. None of this information, including that their president was resigning, was public knowledge. This information was shared because I decided to have some fun blending in with them and just being interested. I told them superficial stuff, talking about the sizzle more than my steak, but I did so with the objective of finding out things that I normally might not. At this stage, I am far removed from being a frontline seller. But as a passing wolf, there were just too many sheep in the yard to not take a few.

You must always practice this because practice makes better. You must also remember that a person's favorite and most familiar topic is oneself. Just ask them. This was first said by Dale Carnegie in one of my favorite books of all times, Winning Friends and Influencing People. It is a must-read if you are dumb enough to consider sales, as it has more to do with people than it does selling. That's the art. And on a person's favorite and most familiar subject, they generally cannot shut up.

I have encountered many, many salespeople and am not ashamed to say that I have been worked by more than a few of them, or so they thought. Although keenly aware in real-time, for me, these encounters usually turn into a fun learning experience. I am proud to say that some of these sales types were working for me while trying to work me. If I am in a bad mood, this is a poor strategy. Those interactions might get you thrown out of my office or an abruptly ended phone conversation. What I want you to understand is that sales professionals typically are always in sales mode, even the weaker types. This is a byproduct of the profession, an occupational hazard of sorts. They often just cannot help themselves. The differences in sales professionals are not that varied, at least not on the surface or initially. The better classes of sales professionals are quite adept at making you feel relaxed to the point that you think you are just having a conversation and not realizing they are probing you and looking for a reason to align with you. They like your sweater or that tie. They may laugh at your attempt at humor. Maybe it is sincere. Maybe not. You are not being sold anything, at least not literally, and usually not for anything tangible or obvious. You are being positioned. You are being subtly disarmed. Flattery is a powerful weapon when done with subtlety. If you were a zebra on the plains of Africa or a warthog in a nearby forest, you are being stalked, intellectually and emotionally. They are observing, gauging, reading, probing. He or she is looking for that opening. If there is an objective, which could be as simple as acceptance, or as pointless as habit, you are in fact being positioned so they can get whatever it is you have. Done correctly and at the proper time, you will happily accommodate. If it is someone on your team, it may be solely for your approval or the hope of being treated like an ally or equal. Transactional sales do not require this kind of cunning or practiced thought, not to mention habit; therefore, the non-transactional sales prize is typically more economically meaningful. That salesperson is looking for an opportunity to strike. These examples describe you as food or prey, you say? Well, if you are a sales prospect and not merely a mouse to play with, just what do you think you are if not food, in a manner of speaking?

You have something of value that may very well serve as sustenance of sorts, or just a win. Or perhaps you are a stone in which to sharpen a sword to him or her. That suit or your shoes may not be as nice as the sales type indicated in the compliment that she just gave you. Perhaps it is, but that wasn't her aim. Appreciation for admiration is a frailty that we almost all fall subject to. But I caution you that it is a part of the stalk and an effective seller's tool. Don't take offense. It is all a part of the lifestyle. And thank you for the contributions that you may have inadvertently given over the years. It's not your fault. You were a means to an end. If this sounds intriguing to do, you may enjoy being dumb enough

Below, I have included a description that I copied directly from Wikipedia* about chameleons, and just above it is the same description slightly altered to describe salespeople, in general. They are strikingly similar.

Compare for yourself:

Salespeople:

Salespeople are a distinctive and can be highly specialized. Salespeople are as old as time itself. They can come from a range of backgrounds and many species can change as needed. Salespeople are often distinguished by their abilities and appearance. A salesperson's eye often wanders, but in aiming at a prey item, they focus forward in coordinating their senses and attention. Salespeople are often adapted for social and professional corporate climbing and visual hunting.

Chameleons[1]

---
[1] Wikipedia 3/14/2016

Chameleons are a distinctive and highly specialized clade of old-world lizards with 202 species described as of June 2015. [1] These species come in a range of colors, and many species have the ability to change colors. Chameleons are distinguished by their zygodactyl feet; their very long, highly modified, rapidly extendable tongue; their swaying gait; [2] and crests or horns on their brow and snout. Most species, the larger ones, have a prehensile tail. Chameleons' eyes are independently mobile, but in aiming at a prey item, they focus forward in coordination, affording the animal stereoscopic vision. Chameleons are adapted for climbing and visual hunting.

Amazingly similar descriptions,

I regard myself as a salesperson, so this by no means is intended to disparage the profession by making an inference that we are dishonest, shallow, or cold-blooded. As I read back this last line, I realize that sadly, this description is very accurate for many, but not most. Sales types are, without question, highly adaptable and generally quite rare. We are also very observant in looking for opportunities. The downside of this trait is that many will bounce from job to job, always thinking the grass next door is greener or that the other company's ice cubes are colder. Not judging, but some may practice on sexual conquests as charm and humor can be problematic in the wrong hands. Some just are always (always) competing for the prize that's available. Others compete because they simply want to feel like they won something, even a potentially toxic prize. Leaving with the prettiest girl in the place, or her phone number, can be quite an ego boost and a victory, of sorts, or so I have been told. It is not that surprising that you may meet successful sellers with disastrous personal lives if they aren't careful with their skills.

Like so many in the animal world, sellers can be extremely messy, like many predators that may leave a lot of meat on the bones. But for sellers, the meat may represent poor follow-up, half-truths, and unfulfilled promises, as they might only cherish the "close" at the expense of everything else. Some enjoy only the hunt and require a lot of clean up, much like the person who walks behind an elephant at the circus with a big broom. Yes. It's shitty work, but usually worth it for the right producer. They may be that person who lives for the hunt and leaves a lot of meat on the carcass because they have grown bored with the kill. Have you ever given your number to someone you seemed to hit it off with only to never receive a phone call? Others are like the hyena that devour bones and usually leaves very little behind. There are successful types who fall into both camps.

Selling skills can indeed be used for bad deeds. Good sellers are not always the best at managing the client once the sale has been made. Like many people, some are better at getting married than they are at staying married. I am not writing a text about being a good spouse or being a player, although some could learn a thing or two by applying effective sales and account management techniques. The next time you encounter a salesperson, and it may be someone who used to be a salesperson and now may be in a leadership role, observe and enjoy. Quite often, they are unconsciously in sales or hunting mode and are completely unaware. If you are considering delving into sales or sales leadership, please consider these qualities coupled with intimate knowledge of the product that you represent. If you don't know your product, these skills may make you simply annoying and ineffective. Great hunters and successful salespeople share another meaningful attribute that I belabored earlier: patience. Type-A sales people usually have learned this important feature the hard way. The problem is that perpetual feeling that "the time is now." Whether that is true or premature, it is potentially problematic to act in haste. Patience will win the day, coupled with staying aware for opportunity. We have all seen that nature show where the young lion prematurely jumps the gun and spoils the hunt.

Part of being a chameleon is staying informed about a lot of things, including current events, in addition to having the good fortune of knowing something of your target's industry. On the first point, having an understanding about current events will give you a sense of what to say, and more importantly, what potentially not say to a client. This is a simple but often overlooked fact. With a Jewish client, don't bring up the settlements. With the black client, don't bring up the police shooting of some unarmed kid. With the Korean client, don't say konnichiwa when you meet them. All obvious points, but these are sharp daggers to kill a sales call. Let's say you know virtually nothing about their business, and you are trying to stoke a conversation. A simple question will often fit the bill. Ask how long they have been in whatever it is. This may lead to asking them what they like about it. You are learning! If you don't have an opportunity to sell this person a thing, you will be better informed in case you meet someone else with a similar business. This is what sales pros do.

If you can be patient enough to understand your client's needs, pain points, dreams, and desires, you will have no choice but to be successful. How you gain this insight is by being a chameleon in any given situation.

Suspects or Prospects?

So, let me start with what is obvious, and that is knowing what a client is. Presuming you know nothing of sales, the easiest interpretation is that a client is a person or entity you are actively conducting and transacting business with. I can almost hear the chorus of duh out there from the many forward-facing selling professionals. This is who a client is not:

- ⟲ Those who will call you to talk about current events routinely, and under the guise of potentially buying something.

- ⟲ The person who will let you pitch anything and everything that is the latest and greatest product in your portfolio just because they like their ass kissed.

- ⟲ It's not necessarily the company that used to buy a lot and often. That doesn't mean you don't continue to pursue.

- ⟲ It's not even that lady who committed to placing that conditional order with you a while ago.

- ⟲ And it is never, ever the person who always says, "Send me your information and we will get back to you," but never does

These are prime examples of prospects, with the last falling firmly within the realm of being a suspect.

There may be a prospect that is so close to doing a deal with you that you can almost taste it almost. Smelling an expertly prepared meal is a far cry from sitting down to eat it. One of my favorite past times (not) is listening to a rep babble on about this person they have on the hook and what it will look like once they land it. To hear them makes that sale sound life altering. You would swear that the salesperson has already cashed the commission check because they are so confident. Well, that fish may be swimming all around the hook, but until they bite or jump onto the boat, they are only a prospect. Maybe a promising prospect, but a prospect, never the less.

The art is converting a suspect into a prospect into a client and the time, energy, and resources that it may require to get them through these stages. If you want to walk their dog or babysit their kids or do whatever it takes, that is completely up to you. Some may make you work so hard that the payoff pales in comparison, ending very anticlimactically. And quite tragically, some may not be worth the care and feeding necessary. Conversely, let's say they may be a very small operation...and so you made very little on the sale itself. It may be worth it in the long-term, as they may see themselves as a walnut that wants to become a mighty oak. But make sure this is truly their dream by way of their actions or you may be shocked to realize late in the game that the dream is yours, and yours alone. The numbers are staggering when considering the amount of times, you may have to call and visit the prospect to make them a client. The pursuit could go on for years. Not everyone has what it takes to chase anything for a week, much less months. The good ones may play the role of the deranged killer in a B-rated slasher movie, calmly walking behind the running, screaming coed (potential client), knowing that it is often a marathon far more times than it is a sprint. What is even more unbelievable are the follow-up statistics that are out there, some of which suggest that if you are just mildly better, where so many falls short, that you would dramatically increase your chances of success over the competition. These are not proprietary points and have been assembled from various public online sources. Some of the statistics include:

02% of sales are made on the first contact

03% of sales are made on the second contact

05% of sales are made on the third contact

80% of sales are made on the fifth to twelfth contact

80% of sales are made on the fifth to twelfth contact (listed twice on purpose!)

48% never follow-up (wow)

25% only make a second follow-up and stop.

ONLY 12% make 3 or more follow-ups!

These numbers are just plain shocking to me. Any successful sales professional will tell you that, unless you are specifically warned or threatened to stay away, a prospect is to be treated and pursued just this side of rendering yourself a stalker, and always tactfully. There are just too many distractions in the world vying for your potential client's time, and the buying funnel is no longer a predictable thing. Not following up is the cornerstone of missed selling opportunities. This is the reason why web programmers have created retargeting. They want a message front and center so they are considered when you are ready to buy. Follow-up is much the same way. You must be front and center in some form or fashion. If you adopt an attitude that they will call you when they are ready, you are very likely to lose. You must ask whether there is a good time to call back. If they say never, it might be best to wait a month. Never leave the question open to your Spidey senses. You will starve.

Suspects are a completely different subject on many, many levels. Unless you are selling a highly unique product, like rocket fuel, rebar, or some other item that serves a narrow market, it is likely that you could conceivably have thousands upon thousands of suspects. Let's consider my business, which is newspaper and website advertising. In my market, there are eleven other daily newspaper competitors and over hundred weekly and monthly publications, all with websites, all chasing the same nickel. This says nothing of the broadcast stations that represent the major networks, the local UHF stations and the hundreds of cable channels that sell commercials. And let's not forget about billboards, many of which are now electronic. Each of these entities is supported by advertising from various companies that were once suspects. Because other media companies were able to match their audience with a need, by selling them time or space, these prospects were converted to clients. But before there was any sort of pitch, they were all suspects. In my world, every single company is a suspect. If you are selling directly to the consumer, every person you meet is a suspect. For business suspects, the second they placed their name in front of their establishment or placed it on the side of a truck, they began promoting their goods and/or services. The beauty of business suspects in general is that they pre-qualify themselves simply by doing this, and existing. But their being suspects makes them just that: a suspect. They are a name and an entity. Your product offerings could be downright offensive or completely miss their target audience. But if you can match them with your wares through qualifying their need with your product, well now you have yourself a prospect. If they buy what you are selling from a competitor, you could conceivably have a chance to sell them also, but they remain a prospect and certainly are quite a distance from being a client, but perhaps considerably further away from being a mere suspect.

The order never deviates: suspect, prospect, client. It is the same as *ready, aim, fire*. You can certainly treat a prospect like a client, but you should not treat a suspect the same way. Call me crazy if you want. What does not help is that often prospects hide in plain sight. Therefore, it is important to carry business cards and never be shy speaking about not only what you do, but also how you help your clients achieve their objectives. Just so I am clear, no one will buy from you simply because you love and are proud of your job. That would be nice, I must say.

chapter 06

There Are No Slow Seasons

Lord knows I have a lot of distractions. As a father of 1.5 adult kids (my plus 30-year-old son is the point 5), I pretty much am left to pursue my passions. I am an avid golfer who keeps clubs in my trunk through the winter in Philadelphia. Hey, 50 and sunny works.

I am also a martial artist who trains five days a week and instructs at two different schools on a volunteer basis. I compete monthly at almost any tournament that I can find within a few hours' drive. I have millions of dollars that I am responsible for and a great deal of pressure. To say that I am a busy person is arguably a huge understatement, but here I am, writing this book.

Despite my distractions, I firmly understand that my work responsibilities are how my pursuits are afforded. Do I squeeze an extra round of golf in here or there? Sure, I do. But never at the expense of compromising what fuels my ability to do so.

Once upon a time I was poor, and let me tell you, I did not like it one bit. I didn't walk to and from school uphill both ways, and I never went hungry or without clean clothes like other kids in my neighborhood, but it was tough. Trust me when I tell you that I am far from being independently wealthy now. Having a good work ethic helped me raise my kids and allowed me opportunities to help other members of my family. My parents worked, and the idea of earning a buck has always appealed to me. Still does.

Unless you are in a sales field where you punch a clock, most other selling positions will award success or even the ability to sustain employment by allowing a fair amount of flexibility and latitude. You have sales meetings and the like, but most often you are held to a number far more than being held to attendance. It can be like college with some courses solely grading on your exams. Where many salespeople get into trouble is not doing what is necessary because the weather is nice, or they would rather be at the beach when they should be being productive. I have seen many come and go because they lack discipline; they slow down because it is the slow season of summer and it is sunny outside. There are no slow seasons in sales. That is a flawed mindset because if you are not harvesting your bounty, you need to be planting seeds for the future...ideally, and always doing both with varying degrees of focus. There should rarely be a day when there isn't something to do to help your productivity.

I am reminded of the ant and the grasshopper story. I am sure that everyone reading this book has heard the story of the ant diligently preparing for winter while it is warm while the grasshopper is jumping around and just enjoying himself. Well, when winter came, you can imagine how the story ended for the free spirited and undisciplined grasshopper. That little tale embodies the differences that can often be found in successful sellers versus the person who wants to smell the flowers just a bit too often. Seasonality isn't a hindrance. It is an opportunity to hone skills, develop and cultivate new clients, and develop and improve new strategies. I am not advocating that one should solely work. Working non-stop not only makes Jane a dull girl; it could make her unbearable. There is a saying that goes something like "It is better to work smart than hard." I absolutely agree that if you can achieve the same results by working smarter, this is the better path to long-term sustainability. If you can get copy approved or a contract signed through technology, why drive over? I absolutely subscribe to playing smart.

Not playing smart is easily accomplished by perpetually not laying the groundwork for future sales or uncovering emerging opportunities. It is too easy to opt and fall victim to distraction. If you are not playing to win you are playing dumb, and dumb is dumb. Jails and unemployment rolls are full of people who just said "f@#k it" right before doing something unimaginably stupid. Saying "hold my beer" is a different book with similar outcomes. In sales, it's saying either and not hustling to be successful. If most people put as much thinking into not working or playing, opting to use this creativeness into how to be better sellers, there would be a lot of more successful salespeople in the world. The statistics are against us. Statistics suggest that if you do nothing, you will likely lose 13% of your business every year. Without any fancy calculations, that equates to 13% of your income. That should be motivating enough.

I have said many times to my people that being a selling professional isn't a job. Selling is and always will be a lifestyle. You are not only thinking about making money while you are trying to make money, you are thinking about opportunities, angles, and pitches. I don't ski, but you are always thinking about making new tracks in the snow. If you are chasing businesses, you are looking at the names on the side of trucks when you are driving. You are considering how that new product that your place rolled out will match with a category of client that you have never pitched. Your significant other is writing down commercials of businesses that they never heard of. It isn't a 9 AM to 5 PM or 5 PM to 2 AM kind of gig. You may not always be pitching, but you are always switched on. There are slower seasons, no doubt.

But there is never a slow season, not for the true players in the sales game.

chapter 07

Your Biggest Opponent is Undefeated

This is one my favorite topics. Time is the most precious commodity that a selling professional has, and by far, is the most fleeting. Everything else is a very close second. Let's look at some of the definitions of time:

As a noun:

The indefinite continued progress of existence and events in the past, present, and future regarded as a whole.

Or

A point of time as measured in hours and minutes past midnight and noon.

As a verb:

To plan, schedule, or arrange when something should happen or be done. These definitions do not quite capture the essence or complexity of time for me. Let's go deeper.

Another web search says: *Time is defined as the duration in which all things happen, or precise instant that something happens.*

These are all quite interesting; however, I don't believe that any get right to the core as it relates to sales. Time for sales is your number one enemy, and as in life, it is undefeated. Every move and action that you undertake as a sales professional must be done with one eye on the clock. There is always a budget/goal to meet within a period time, a publishing deadline, time for materials, or a client's specific time to accommodate. The demand for what is a selling professional's life blood, time, is never-ending. It is incumbent upon you to maximize every second because it is unrelenting. Sure, there are things you must do to keep your boss happy, with meetings and so forth so that they can answer their boss's inquiries to show that they are involved. You want them informed. If they can help or advise, great. Your goal is to eliminate anything that gets in the way of making money. That statement is a hard stop. This doesn't mean you do not fulfill your obligations to your clients.

There are always a few things to be done. You want to get those things done and go get the money. It is a simple formula. There will be other reps who want to chit-chat about last night's game or how their kid needs braces, or how they just got back from Vegas. It is all a waste of your time. Maintain relationships at work, but don't allow those conversations or relationships to impede upon your success. Again. full stop.

The question you must ask yourself is how much your time is worth? If you do the math, you would be amazed just how much that is. You don't have it to spare, because your aim is to increase the value of your time, which translates to more money. Re-read that line. Do the meetings you have to do and kibitz with your work friends. Your goal is to let none of it get in your way because your enemy is ever-present and undefeated.

Tick-tock.

chapter 08

Is it Speed Dating or Courtship?

Yes, is the answer to both. We did something some years ago. My company did a week-long seminar, and we invited companies to come in and learn about the wonders of advertising. The program was essentially hosting companies that do little or no business with us. We invited them to a venue to lay out the fundamentals of a sustained campaign with the keys to any successful promotional campaign: audience and frequency. It was a success.

The program itself involved identifying the organization's primary target audience, a desirable and attractive visual display area with brightly-lit kiosks, and an opening presentation by yours truly, which was then followed by a short video, an assumed close by me, and on to the hard close by the reps and the potential clients. I had to present 37 times to new perspective advertisers over a 5-day period. Narcissist that I am, I loved every second of it. The exercise was the ultimate assumptive/presumptive sale. What I tried to explain to my people was that this was very much like how we operated in the retail industry. In advertising, we tend to court our clients and potentials while trying to detect a buying signal. In retail, you assume a buying signal is that person saying hello back to you. It is the fine art and ability of establishing a connection as quickly as possible. They don't have to love you; they simply need to tolerate you and your ability to lead them to where they want to go. This was a stark reminder of when I moved from retail into advertising, which is completely in the reverse order that I previously spoke of. At first, it was difficult, as I was accustomed to a much higher occurrence of yes versus no, having been an unwitting and effective "ABC" (always be closing) person throughout my retail career. In fact, the last year and a half that I was in retail, I had to go back to a selling position with management responsibilities (as an assistant manager) as prior to that I was a store manager and rarely sold on the floor having done my time and had earned my stripes. I was the youngest store manager in the company's history, and as the national electronic retailers slowly began to dominate the market, we were closing stores. There were managers in the business longer than I had been on the planet, much less in the business. Within six months, I was the company's top producer, and I hadn't been on the selling floor full-time in three years. It was great to see that I could still walk it like I talk it. I never lost my ability to focus on making an instantaneous connection with a prospect. This is a skill you should always work on. Talk to strangers. Practice on your neighbors or anyone who presents an opportunity. Remember that when you are really selling, you are positioning yourself as much as you are your wares. But is this positioning speed-dating, or a courtship? Of course, it depends on what you are selling, and in other times, it depend on the given set of circumstances.

chapter 09

Mr. Support Person...

Let me be clear...you need the team. Selling and executing without support usually falls short.

One of my favorite movies and scenes is from A Few Good Men with Jack Nicholson and Tom Cruise. It tells the story of an opportunistic lawyer doing his time in the Navy Jag Corp who gets thrown into a real murder case that involves a legendary military leader. The dramatic ending is really the movie, and the first two odd hours are merely a setup. Some of you who are familiar are probably thinking of the *"You can't handle the truth"* line. It is after Jack says that part that I personally enjoy. It is him challenging those without his responsibilities or skillset. In my business, like pretty much every other, revenue is what drives the engine. There are a lot of pieces that go into generating our revenue from different departments. All play a vital role. Does a waiter play a role in a restaurant? A stewardess on an airline? I say absolutely. All are important to the success of each endeavor. But it is the skills of the taxi operator, the chef, and the pilot that are the most critical. It certainly is not the waiter telling the chef how to prepare the house special, that's for sure. In many businesses, there are people in support departments that are under the belief that it is they who know how best to close a sale or do the thing that most supports the business. And, of course, every "home office" expert has an opinion and invariably a criticism. Although many are very skilled and talented at their discipline, they would starve to death if they had to rely on selling skills to eat. It can be insulting and galling. But these people are important to your mission, and it is imperative that you utilize their abilities to accomplish your mission. As annoying as it may be, when what seems to be Monday-morning quarterbacking your victories and defeats, you must remain professional, and most of all…wait for it…be patient. Find the humor in it, with a lot of deep breathing. They generally are trying to be helpful.

So, the next time that fill-in-the-blank department person offers to give an opinion or to criticize under the flag of helping, just do what I do. Think of Jack telling Tom or asking Lt. Weinberg if they are willing to do it. I would never do this, of course. But it is fun to entertain the thought. Generally, a salesperson could never do their jobs either. It takes a chorus and you play a part. Too many sales types think that their part is more important and at the expense of all else. I once upon a time thought in this manner, which was a mistake.

Listen and consider whatever advice that is offered. It doesn't mean that you should follow it. You may learn something that you had not considered, even from a non-seller.

conclusion

Go Make Some Money!

The big question is whether you are interested in selling for a living? Are you selling what you do now, even if it isn't direct sales? Are you dumb enough? It is a difficult and frustrating way to make a buck. But it can be lucrative and tied directly to how hard you work at it. Luck matters: the harder you work, the luckier you will be. This has been proven time and again. If you are a selling professional currently, and have been for an appreciable amount of time, you are keenly aware of your shortcomings. Perhaps it is cold calling or appointment setting. Maybe you can improve on closing or give more focus to follow-up.

Whatever it may be, your goal should be to take your weakest element and work on it so you can improve. This may prove difficult as it may feel like you are trying to make a cube into a circle at first. What that means is every time you cut a corner off; you make more corners. But what you are doing is making it smoother and getting to your goal of making it round. This will require focus and commitment to get there. You can do it if you try.

To summarize a few earlier points:

- You have been selling your entire life. Pay attention to when you are selling now, even if selling is not your profession. Just because there is no financial consideration matters not.

- You shouldn't be afraid of selling. Be afraid when you don't do the things to make you successful.

- If you are a minority or a woman, don't allow your sensitivities to get in the way of your mission.

- Part of being a chameleon is paying attention to what is going on in the world. You should also endeavor to be able to blend into any crowd.

- Know the difference between suspects, prospects, and clients.

- Take advantage of slower periods. These times offer opportunity. Be the ant.

- Court *and* speed date. Both are needed skillsets.

- Respect and utilize your support system, even if they challenge or second guess you or your results.

- Remember to breathe.

Thank you for taking the time to read my thoughts. I hope that you learned a thing or two, and that you are now dumb enough.

www.ingramcontent.com/pod-product-compliance
Lightning Source LLC
Chambersburg PA
CBHW050256220526
45465CB00002B/701